CW01667394

Genova 2014

Happy Birthday

From [illegible]

Laura Rangoni

Perfumes and flavours of Liguria

THE REAL LIGURIAN KITCHEN

Edizioni Servizi Editoriali

Disegni: Carlotta Casa
Foto di: Carmelo Marino

Ligurpress s.r.l.
Via Luigi Canepa, 11/L-R
16165 Genova
Tel.: 010 8605005
Fax: 010 8606090
e-mail: info@ligurpress.it
www.ligurpress.it

ISBN
9788864060408

Sauces and Gravy

Sughi e Salse

AGGIADA

Serves 4

8 cloves garlic
1 cup white wine vinegar
1 cup bread crumbs
1/2 cup of dry white wine
Salt

Using a pestle & mortar work the cloves of garlic until it becomes a paste. Soak bread crumbs in vinegar, remove excess liquid add to garlic paste and mix. Add a pinch of salt and whit wine. Place in small saucepan and bring to boil for a few minutes until the sauce is thickened.

AGLIATA DI VESSALICO

Serves 4

Egg yolk
2 cloves garlic
1 cup extra virgin olive oil
Salt

Crush garlic with pestle & mortar until of creamy consistency. Add a pinch of salt and mix in egg yolk. Slowly add in olive oil to mixture (as if making mayonnaise). This sauce should have a thick consistency. Salt and serve.

MACHETTO

SERVES 4

500 gr. of small fresh anchovies
1 cup of extra virgin olive oil
5 tbsp coarse Salt

Carefully wash and remove all entrails of anchovies as well as the heads leaving only the fillets. Place a first layer in a large bowl of glass and cover the layer with a spoonful of coarse salt and continue layers in this manner to top of bowl. Place a heavy weight on top of layers so that they remain well pressed- Let stand for a month in a dry and cool place. After blending the anchovy and salt mixture put in jam jars and top with good oil. Before using the mixture blend a spoonful of oil into it.

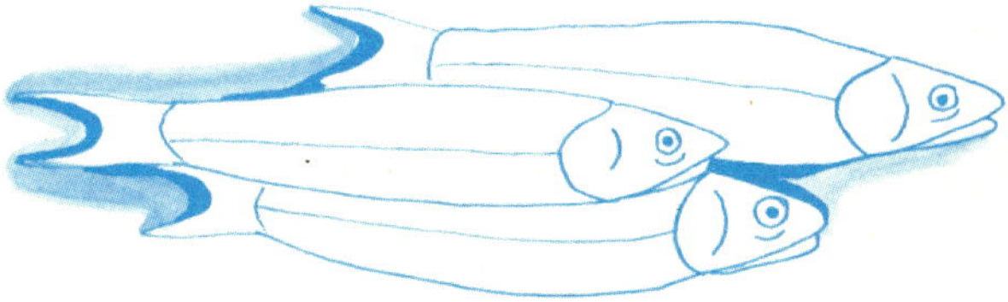

GARLIC AND BASIL SAUCE
PESTO
SERVES 4

40-50 small fresh basil leaves
1 spoonful grated Sardinian ewe's milk cheese
4 spoonful grated parmesan cheese
50 gr. pine nuts
1 cup of olive oil
5-6 cloves garlic
Salt

The traditional method for making pesto is using a mortar, but often nowadays, people use a blender, Blend the basil, pine nuts, garlic cloves and salt and beat at length with the pestle till a smooth mixture is obtained. Add ewe's milk cheese and mix, then add parmesan cheese and mix again. Finally pour a thread of oil onto mixture and mix until all is well blended.

GARLIC SAUCE FROM PENTEMA
PESTO D'AGLIO DI PENTEMA
SERVES 4

4 cloves garlic
50 gr. pine nuts
50 gr. parmesan, grated, fresh
4 spoons cream
1 cup of olive oil
Salt

Blend garlic and pine nuts until well mixed, Add parmesan, mix well and add cream. Mix well add salt. Slowly add oil while stirring constantly, This sauce can be used for pasta, boiled vegetables, etc.

GENOESE SAUCE
SALSA ALLA GENOVESE
SERVES 4

8 stoned olives
1 tbsp vinegar
1/2 cup salted capers
yolk of boiled egg
1/2 cup extra virgin olive oil
salt/pepper
sprig of parsley
1/2 cup bread crumbs
1/2 lemon
1 clove garlic
50 gr. pine nuts
1 brined anchovy

Soak breadcrumbs in vinegar, until well soaked, drain off excess liquid, Rinse excess salt off capers and drain. Place capers, olives, garlic, anchovies, pine nuts, parsley, breadcrumbs, egg yolk, salt and pepper in bowl, mix in juice of lemon, slowly pour in olive oil and mix constantly until smooth.

MARINARA SAUCE
SALSA MARINARA
SERVES 4

6 salted anchovies
2 cloves of garlic
4 spoons tomato paste
4 spoons extra virgin olive oil
1 spoon whit whine
Salt and pepper

Wash and remove bones from anchovies. Blend anchovies with garlic until creamy . Add tomato paste, wine, salt, pepper and mix. Slowly dribble oil into mixture stirring constantly.

NUT SAUCE
SALSA DI NOCI
Serves 4

250 gr. walnuts
25 gr. curd (prescinseua)
50 gr. pine nuts
1 clove garlic
4 tablespoons extra virgin olive oil
1/4 cup fresh breadcrumbs
1/2 glass of milk

Soak breadcrumbs in milk, when soaked remove excess liquid. Blend together breadcrumbs, walnuts, clove of garlic, salt and pine nuts. Mix well. Add curd and again mix . Slowly dribble oil into mixture, stirring constantly.

PINE-NUT SAUCE
SALSA DI PINOLI
Serves 4

50 gr. pine -nuts
50 gr. fresh breadcrumbs
1 glass of extra virgin olive oil
1 spoon vinegar
Salt

Soak breadcrumbs in vinegar, when soaked remove excess liquid. Blend breadcrumbs and pine nuts together. Add salt and spoonful of vinegar, mix. Slowly dribble oil into mixture, stirring constantly until smooth.

MUSSEL SAUCE
SUGO DI MUSCOLI
SERVES 4

1 kg. mussels
2 salted anchovies
1/2 glass extra virgin oil
3 ripe tomatoes
4 cloves of garlic
1/2 glass white wine
salt/pepper
Sprig of parsley

Thoroughly wash and clean the mussels Place cleaned mussels in large saucepan with oil, crushed garlic and finely chopped parsley. When mussels open, add wine and continue cooking for a little while longer. Remove mussels from pan and remove mussels from shells, filter the liquid from pan to remove any particles. Roughly chop anchovy fillets. Place in pan, cook on low heat until melted. Add chopped tomatoes, increase heat and cook until a sauce is obtained. Add mussels and the filtered stock, cook until sauce has thickened, season with salt and pepper.

WALNUT GRAVY
SUGO DI NOCI
SERVES 4

500 gr. walnuts
6 tablespoons extra virgin olive oil
Sprig parsley
4 tablespoons grated pecorino cheese
10 gr. pine nuts
1 clove garlic
5 sticks marjoram
Salt

Place nuts in boiling water for approximately 5 minutes, so as to facilitate the removal of outer skin. Blend together with pine nuts, garlic parsley and marjoram. When mixed, add pecorino cheese and dribble in oil until well mixed. Add salt as required.

FISH GRAVY
SUGO DI PESCE
SERVES 4

100 gr. fresh pieces, head and bones
4 tablespoons extra virgin olive oil
2 ripe tomatoes
4 tablespoons flour
10 gr. dried mushrooms
1 sprig parsley
50g pine nuts
1 clove garlic
1 onion
1 sprig rosemary
1 carrot
salt/pepper

Finely chop carrot, onion, rosemary, parsley and garlic. Gently fry mixture until golden, add fish parts. Having soaked mushrooms in water until softened , drain and chop finely before adding to pan. Allow to cook for 10 minutes, pour a little wine and then add cubed tomatoes. Sieve the gravy, put into another pan and thicken with the flour. Add salt and pepper, finely chopped pine nuts and mix.

Appetizers and single dishes

Antipasti e piatti unici

HERBED MONTEROSSO ANCHOVIES

ACCIUGHE DI MONTEROSSO ALLE ERBE

SERVES 4

500 gr. anchovies
50 gr. butter
Sprigs of parsley
1 bay leaf
2 cloves
1 onion
1 clove of garlic
rosemary
thyme
juice 1/2 lemon
1/2 glass white wine
1 tbsp flour

Clean and fillet anchovies. Boil them in water and white wine in equal parts with the herbs (thyme - bay leaf - cloves - parsley) the sliced onion, crushed clove garlic. Bring to boil for 10 minutes. When cooked remove anchovies from stock, taking care not to break them. Arrange on serving dish. Keep warm. Heat saucepan with butter and add flour diluted with two glasses of the sieved stock, mix continuously and when sauce is thickened add juice of lemon.

Pour over anchovies and serve. Serve dish with toasted garlic bread.

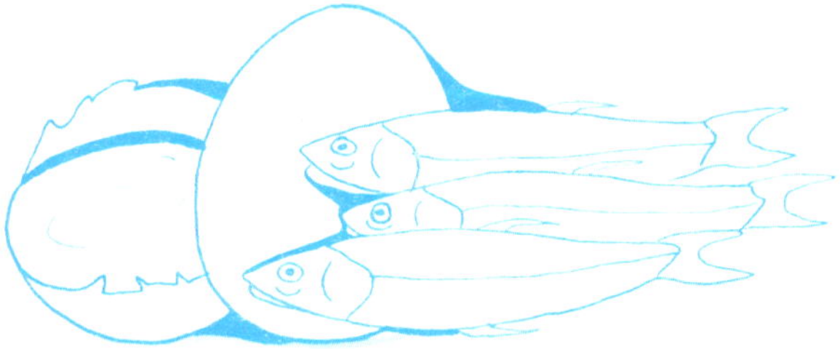

MARINATED ANCHOVIES

ACCIUGHINE MARINATE

SERVES 4

800 gr. small, fresh anchovies
Juice of 2 lemons
1/4 glass dry white wine
1/2 glass extra virgin olive oil
1 clove garlic
Sprig of parsley
Salt

Clean and fillet anchovies. Place open flat anchovies in deep dish. Mix lemon juice, wine, oil, salt, crushed garlic and finely chopped parsley. Pour mix over anchovies, let sit at least 2 hours.

MONEGLIA APPETIZER

ANTIPASTO DI MONEGLIA

SERVES 4

500 gr. fish, small
100 gr. flour
1/2 glass white wine vinegar
1 glass white wine
Cooking oil
2 cloves of garlic. sliced
1 sliced onion
7-8 leaves of sage
salt

Clean and fillet fish, dredge and fry fish in very hot oil. When cooked pat dry with kitchen absorbent roll to remove excess oil before placing in a large bowl. Cover fish with vinegar, wine, salt, pepper, garlic clove, onion and sage. Leave to marinate for at least 2 hours. Remove fish from liquid and serve.

CONDIGLIONE DELLA RIVIERA DEI FIORI

SERVES 4

2 kg. tomatoes
1/2 yellow pepper
1 cucumber
2 cloves garlic
Basil
1/2 glass extra virgin oil
2 small onions
oregano
1/4 cup black olives stoned
50 gr. tuna
1 hard boiled egg
2 salted anchovies
salt and pepper

Slice not too ripe tomatoes and cucumber, add 1/2 yellow pepper cut into thin strips , coarsely chopped basil leaves, oregano, the washed filleted anchovies cut into pieces, thinly sliced onions, crushed cloves garlic. Mix together and add roughly mashed boiled egg, the stoned olives and tuna. Sprinkle with salt and pepper and pour a little oil. Mix well before servingr.

FARINATA

SERVES 4

250 gr. chick-pea flour
1/2 glass extra virgin olive oil
3/4 litre water
Salt
Black pepper

Prepare batter by mixing chick-pea flour and water. Beat mixture with whisk until smooth and all hard lumps are smoothed out, let rest for at least 4 hours. Then oil a shallow baking tin and pour liquid. Preheat oven to 200°, place in oven and let cook for 1/2 an hour or at least until golden brown. Before serving sprinkle with salt and freshly ground black pepper.

FOCACCIA

SERVES 4

200 gr. flour
30 gr.. yeast
1/2 glass of extra virgin olive oil
Salt

Blend yeast in some warm water and add to the flour to obtain a smooth soft mixture. Leave the dough to rise in a warm place for 1 ? hour. Then spread the dough out evenly over base of oiled shallow baking pan. Thickness not to exceed 2cm. Sprinkle salt dribble a little oil over all the foccaccia surface. Bake in moderate oven (180° C9 for at least 20 minutes.

CHEESE FOCACCIA (RECCO ORIGIN)

FOCACCIA COL FORMAGGIO

SERVES 4

50 gr. flour
300 gr. "formaggetta" (cheese)
1/2 glass extra virgin oil
Salt

On a floured board, mix flour, a tablespoon salt and enough water to obtain a soft dough. Cover dough with teatowel and let it rest for about 1/2 hr. Shape the dough into two not too thin discs. Place one of the discs on an oiled pan spread with cheese cut into cubes, then place second disc over top. Lightly prick the foccaccia surface with fork, drizzle lightly with olive oil, sprinkle with salt and cook in a hot oven at 200°C for at least 20 minutes.

SEA BISCUITS (CRACKERS)
GALLETTE
SERVES 4 TO 6

1 kg. flour
50 gr. fresh yeast
2 litres water
A pinch of salt

Blend yeast in some warm water and then add to flour, mix , add a pinch of salt and remaining water to obtain a dough. Leave dough in a warm place for at least 1/4 hr to let rise. Knead dough , then divide into small balls, spread out each ball with rolling pin. Leave for another 3/4 hr. Using appropriate mould shape into typical form. Bake in a preheated oven to 220°C for at least 30 minutes. Let stand to cool and dry out. Can keep for a couple of months.

SEAFOOD SALAD
INSALATA DI MARE
SERVES 4

200 gr. mussels
400 gr. razor-shell clam
200 gr. prawns
200 gr. baby octopus
2/3 tablespoons basil leaves
1 clove garlic
1/2 cup extra virgin olive oil
1 lemon
salt and pepper
2/3 finely chopped parsley

Clean and cook baby octopus in boiling water for at least 1/4 hr. In meantime, clean and steam open mussels. Wash the razor-shell clams under running water (making sure that all sand is removed). Cook in hot water for 5 minutes. Boil the prawns in hot water for a couple of minutes also. Allow all ingredients to cool. Cut into small pieces and dress with lemon juice, finely chopped parsley and clove garlic, salt and pepper and olive oil. Garnish with fresh basil leaves.

RICE SALAD À LA MARINARA
INSALATA DI RISO ALLA MARINARA

SERVES 4

400 gr. rice
400 gr. prawn tails
400 gr. mussels
400 gr. cockles and hard-shell clams
4 anchovy fillets
1/2 lemon
2/3 tbsp parsley
1/2 cup white wine, dry
4 tbsp extra virgin olive oil
salt and pepper

Cook the shrimps in boiling water for a couple of minutes, drain, shell and chop coarsely. Brush the clams and cockleshells clean, place in a large pan, cover with white wine and cook until open. Once open, remove the mussel meat from shell ; discard any unopened shells, and reserve. Continue cooking until the sauce begins to thicken. Once thickened, filter.

Cook rice in salted water, drain and pass under running cold water. Drain well and place the rice on serving dish with shrimps and mussel meat. Blend the anchovies, parsley, lemon juice and a couple of spoons of the thickened sauce. Sprinkle with freshly ground pepper and dribble oil onto mixture. Pour this sauce onto rice, stir and serve.

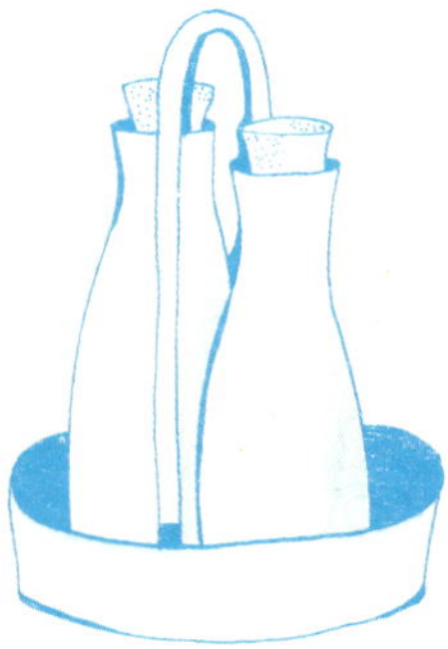

BABY OCTOPUS WITH SAUCE
MOSCARDINI AL SUGHETTO

SERVES 4

2 kg. baby octopus
1 onion
250 gr. tomato
1/2 cup parsley
Salt and pepper
1 clove garlic
30 gr. dried mushrooms
Sprig of rosemary
1/2 glass extra virgin olive oil
Fried sliced bread

Finely chop parsley, rosemary, onion and clove garlic and sauté for a couple of minutes until softened. Add the mushrooms previously soaked in warm water, drained and chopped. Add tomatoes, salt and pepper. Stir and allow to cook for at least 20 minutes, adding, when necessary a couple of spoonsful of the filtered mushroom water. Add the cleaned octopus and continue cooking, covered, at low heat for another 45 minutes. Place the fried bread slices on a serving dish, top with the octopus and the sauce poured over and around. Serve hot.

PANISSA GENOVESE

SERVES 4

300 gr. chick pea flour
1/2 glass extra virgin olive oil
Salt
1 litre water
4-5 onions

Pour water in a saucepan and bring to boil, reduce heat and fold in the chickpea flour. Stir constantly over heat until smooth: continually stir for at least an hour. Place the mixture in a bowl and let it cool. Cut into wedges. Slice onions and sauté in a little oil. When onions are a golden colour add the panissa wedges, salt and after a few minutes, serve.

ANDREA DORIA PIZZA
PISCIALANDREA
SERVES 4

500 gr. white flour
1/2 glass milk
4 salted anchovies
1/2 cup black olives, stoned
1/2 cup pressed basil leaves
1/2 glass extra virgin olive oil
25 gr. yeast, fresh
2 onions
400g can tomatoes
5 cloves garlic
A pinch marjoram

Dissolve yeast in a little lukewarm water and then add to the flour. Add salt, milk and a tbsp of oil. Work to make a soft dough. Leave in a warm place for an hour to rise or double the size. Meanwhile, sauté the thinly sliced onions until golden brown, add the washed and chopped anchovies, the drained can tomatoes, basil and salt. Let cook for 15 minutes or until sauce thickens. Roll out dough and line greased pan, top with stoned olives cut in half, the garlic cloves, then spread the tomato and anchovy sauce and sprinkle with oregano and salt. Bake in hot oven at 180° C for at least 30 minutes. Serve hot.

SARDINES WITH BASIL SAUCE
SARDINE CON SALSA AL BASILICO
SERVES 4

16 sardines
1 tbsp chopped basil
6 tbsp extra virgin olive oil
1 tbsp chopped parsley
1 tbsp salted capers
Salt and pepper

Place the finely chopped parsley and basil, the washed capers in a bowl together with the oil and mix. Season with salt and pepper and dress the sardines previously washed, filleted and grilled, with this basil sauce. Serve this dish with toasted garlic bread.

PASQUALINA CAKE
TORTA PASQUALINA
SERVES 4

For the pastry:
400 gr. flour
4 tbsp extra virgin olive oil

For the filling:
1 kg. silverbeet
500 gr. quagliata (curdled cheese) (prescinseua)
1 onion
1/2 glass extra virgin olive oil
20 gr. dried mushroom
1 glass liquid carton cream
6 hard boiled eggs
100 gr. seasoned grated parmesan cheese
4 fresh eggs
sprig marjoram
Salt and pepper

This recipe is one of the many for this dish. Mix the flour with water, oil and salt and continue mixing until the mixture is soft and smooth. Divide it into 8-10 balls. Let stand, covered by a cloth, for a couple of hours.
Tradition dictates that the balls should be 33 ,one to mark each year of Christ's life. Wash the beet greens well, strip away the tough ribs and slice into very thin strips. Cook for about 10 minutes in a shallow pan with little oil, salt and pepper. Remove from pan, drain excess water, stir in parmesan cheese, salt , a sprinkle of marjoram and a couple of spoonsful of prescinseau mixed with carton cream. Soak mushrooms in warm water, drain all excess water. Heat pan with a little oil add finely copped onion and the mushrooms and sauté for at least 15 minutes. Remove from pan and reserve.

Next, beat four eggs with grated parmesan cheese, the prescinseau and remaining carton cream. Mix thoroughly and pour onto the silverbeet, mix until amalgamated and season.
Grease a 30cm base x 3cm high baking tin. Take half of the 8-10 dough balls and roll them out paper thin one at a time . Lay down the pastry sheets enough to line base and sides of the prepared baking tin, making sure they overlap the tin. Drizzle all but the last one with oil. Spread the beet greens over the sheets and then spread the presinseau mixture over the greens.
Use the back of a spoon to press out 6 depressions on the top of the cheese mixture and place a hard boiled egg in each one. Drizzle each with a little oil, and season with salt and pepper.
Take the remaining dough ball and roll out as previously. Lay them down over the pie, oiling them well and making sure they overlap the baking tin, Try to keep them separate by blowing a little air between the layers with the help of a straw. Then press the overlapping edges of the layers together so as to obtain a border for the pie. Again tradition has it that the initials of the head of the household be pressed into the crust.
Bake in hot oven (190°) for at least half an hour or until the pastry turns a golden colour.

CIUPPIN

SERVES 4

1.5 kg. fish (eels, anglers, congers, octopus, cuttlefish, redfish, etc).
1 onion
pinch of oregano
1 carrot
5 tbsp extra virgin olive oil
sprig of parsley
4 ripe tomatoes
2 cloves garlic
1 glass white wine
Toasted bread slices
salt and pepper

Clean all the fish, remove fish bones and cut into pieces. Put heads and tails aside. Meanwhile, heat oil in large earthenware casserole, add finely chopped celery, carrot and onion, sauté and when golden brown, add a glass of white wine and let it evaporate. Add oregano, finely chopped parsley and garlic. Then add tomato pulp, stir all ingredients, cover and cook for at least ? hr. Add all the fish, season with salt and pepper, cover and continue cooking on a low heat for at least another 2 hrs. When fish is cooked, filter the soup with strainer and mash. Serve hot with toasted bread slices.

BASIL SAUCE CREPES
CREPES AL PESTO
SERVES 4

Crepes:
150 gr. flour
2 eggs
1 glass milk

Sauce:
1/2 glass extra virgin olive oil
4 tbsp milk
Bechamel sauce
50gr. grated parmesan cheese
1 clove garlic
Salt and pepper

Sift flour, stir in eggs, milk and salt. Beat (blend or process) all ingredients until smooth. Cover and let rest for at least an hour. Place lightly greased non-stick frying pan over low heat. Pour 2 or 3 table-spoons of batter onto pan, brown lightly underneath; turn, brown other side. Turn onto plate and let cool. Repeat with remaining batter.
Combine pesto (basil sauce), bechamel, a spoonful of oil, grated parmesan cheese, 4 tablespoons of milk, finely chopped clove garlic, freshly ground pepper and salt in a bowl and mix together. Spread a layer of the basil bechamel onto an over tray, top with a layer of crepes, one slightly over the other, spread another thinner layer of basil bechamel and repeat with remaining crepes. Top last layer with grated cheese. Bake in hot oven at 180° c for 30 minutes.

REEF FETTUCCINE
FETTUCCINE ALLO SCOGLIO
SERVES 4

500 gr. egg fettuccine
sprig of parsley
200 gr. small squid
chilli peppers at will
200 gr. crayfish
1/2 glass white wine
300 gr. mussels
4 tbsp extra virgin olive oil
200 gr. clams
salt
200 gr. Dublin bay prawns
4 cloves garlic

Heat oil in frying pan, add crushed garlic clove and a little chilli peppers. Cook for a few seconds then add a drop of wine, the small squid, the crayfish, parsley and a pinch of salt. Cook for another 15 minutes. Heat oil in another pan add the mussels and clams, the crushed garlic and remaining wine. Add the pasta (fettuccine) to large saucepan of salted boiling water, boil, uncovered until jest tender, drain. Stir pasta into pan with small squid, crayfish and prawns, Pour onto serving dish and garnish with the shell-fish and finely chopped parsley.

"BUTTERFLY" PASTA WITH PEAS
GASSE (FARFALLE) CON I PISELLI

SERVES 4

For dough:
500 gr. flour
2 eggs
50 gr. grated parmesan cheese
Salt

Sauce:
250 gr. shelled peas
1 onion
2 ladles stock
50 gr. grated parmesan cheese.
100 gr. baked ham
2 tbsp extra virgin olive oil
60 gr. butter

Make mound with the flour on your work surface. Add pinch of salt, the grated cheese and the eggs. Work the ingredients together till you have a smooth dough. Knead the dough for at least 20 minutes. Flour the work surface and roll out the dough to a 3mm thickness. Let it dry for a couple of minutes. Cut into 4cm wide strips and again into 6cm long rectangles. Once cut, crimp the centre together in order to form the bow-tie shape. Cover the "farfalle" pasta with teatowel and let dry for a couple of hours.

In meantime, heat oil and 20g butter in saucepan, add the finely chopped onion and diced ham. Stir occasionally over heat for about 5 minutes then add shelled peas. Stir until combined and let cook for another ten minutes. Add a ladle of stock, salt and continue cooking uncovered until mixture is ready. If necessary add other stock.

Add the "farfalle" pasta gradually to large saucepan of boiling salted water, boil, uncovered, for about ten minutes or until tender. Drain and place on serving dish. Stir in the peas and ham sauce, top with hot melted butter and abundant grated parmesan cheese.

CRAYFISH LASAGNE
LASAGNE AI GAMBERI
Serves 4

For dough:
300 gr. flour
3 eggs
A pinch of salt

Sauce:
Bechamel sauce
1 onion
1 carrot
1 celery stalk
4-5 tbsp extra virgin olive oil
400 gr. canned peeled tomatoes
300 gr. shelled prawns
a little butter
50 gr. grated cheese
salt and chilli pepper

Mix the flour and eggs on the work surface till you have a smooth firm dough. Let stand for at least half an hour. Then roll out dough into a thin sheet. With the aid of a cutter, cut into 10cm strips. Once the dough is all cut, let it dry out for another half an hour.
Meanwhile sauté in oil, the chopped celery, carrot and onion, and canned tomatoes. Let cook. Then add shelled prawns and season with salt and a pinch of chilli pepper. Allow to cook another 5-6 minutes.
Cook the lasagne in salted boiling water. Boil rapidly, uncovered for a couple of minutes, drain and place lasagne on a teatowel to dry out.
Lightly grease oven tray. Layer lasagne strips, then spread bechamel sauce and top with prawn sauce. Repeat procedure with remaining lasagne and sauce until all is used up. Top with bechamel sauce and sprinkle grated parmesan cheese. Preheat oven to 180°C and bake for at least 30 minutes or until golden brown.

BASIL SAUCE LASAGNE
LASAGNE AL PESTO

SERVES 4

For dough:

600 gr. flour
6 eggs

For sauce:

10 cloves garlic
1/3 cup pine nuts
1/2 cup crushed walnuts
1 small bunch basil leaves
Bechamel sauce
1/2 glass extra virgin olive oil
100g butter
100 gr. pecorino cheese
100 gr. parmesan cheese
Salt and pepper

Mix the flour and the eggs on work surface till you have a smooth, firm dough. Let stand for at least half an hour. Roll out dough into a thin sheet. Cut the pastry sheets into 10cm squares. Once dough is all cut, let it dry out for another half an hour.
Finely chop up (or use food processor) garlic, basil, walnuts and pine nuts. Transfer mixture into mortar/bowl add oil in slow stream and grated cheese. Continue stirring so as to mix all ingredients. Melted butter is an option making pesto mixture thicker and more savoury.
Prepare bechamel sauce by melting butter, in medium saucepan, over low heat. Add flour, gradually stir in a little milk. Stir constantly until sauce is smooth and thickened somewhat.
Cook the lasagne in salted boiling water. Boil rapidly, uncovered, for a couple of minutes, drain and set on clean cloth. Lightly grease oven tray. Set down a layer of pasta, then a layer of bechamel sauce, then spread the pesto and sprinkle with grated cheese. Continue alternating the lasagne, the bechamel sauce and the pesto till all is used up. Top with bechamel sauce an sprinkle with grated parmesan cheese.
Preheat oven to 180°C and cook for at least 10-15 minutes or until golden brown.

SILK HANDKERCHIEFS
MANDILLI DI SAEA (FAZZOLETTI DI SETA)
SERVES 4

For the dough:
500 gr. flour
2 tbsp bran
4 eggs

For sauce:
1 tbsp olive oil
4 tbsp pesto (basil sauce)
100 gr. grated parmesan cheese
Salt and pepper

Make mound wit sifted flour and bran on work surface, scoop out a well in the middle and place eggs and pinch of salt into the hole. Work eggs and flour together to make a smooth dough. Knead dough until smooth, firm and quite elastic. Roll out dough into thin sheet, cut into 20cm squares.
Add the squares gradually, 1 or 2 at a time, in a large saucepan of boiling water, adding a tbsp of oil to keep squares from sticking together. Boil rapidly until tender, drain. Serve hot with basil sauce. Add grated parmesan cheese and sprinkle freshly ground pepper.

MES-CIUA

SERVES 4

200 gr. White beans (cannelloni)
200 gr. Chick peas
50 gr. Wheat
1/2 glass extra virgin olive oil
4 slices toasted bread
Salt and black pepper

Soak chick-peas and wheat in lukewarm water for 24 hours and beans for 12 hours. Place chickpeas, wheat and water used for soaking into a deep saucepan. Bring to boil and let cook for at least 3 hours.
Pour beans and water used for soaking in another deep saucepan, bring to boil and let cook for at least 1 1/2 hours. Then pour chickpeas, wheat and white beans into single deep saucepan, stir, add salt and allow to boil for another ten minutes. In each dish place slice of toasted bread, pour soup on top, drizzle a little oil and a generous serving of freshly ground pepper. Serve hot.

GENOESE VEGETABLE SOUP
MINESTRONE ALLA GENOVESE

SERVES 4

500 gr. white potatoes
250 gr. kidney beans
Bunch of silverbeet
1 piece of cabbage
Carrot
4 zucchini
1/2 glass extra virgin olive oil
100 gr. grated parmesan cheese
150 gr. French beans
1 small eggplant
Bunch of borage greens
Celery stalk
Onion
200 gr. short pasta
4 tbsp pesto
Salt and pepper

Chop up all the greens except potatoes, the egg plant, the tomato and beans. Bring to boil in large pot at least 2 litres salted water. When water is boiling add all the ingredients and cook for at least an hour. Then, with a ladle, remove potatoes, egg plant, tomato and mash with fork. Return vegetables to pot and add oil and pasta. Continue cooking until pasta is tender. Turn off heat. Add pesto sauce, stir and let rest for a least 15 minutes. Serve and add a stream of oil, pepper and grated parmesan cheese.

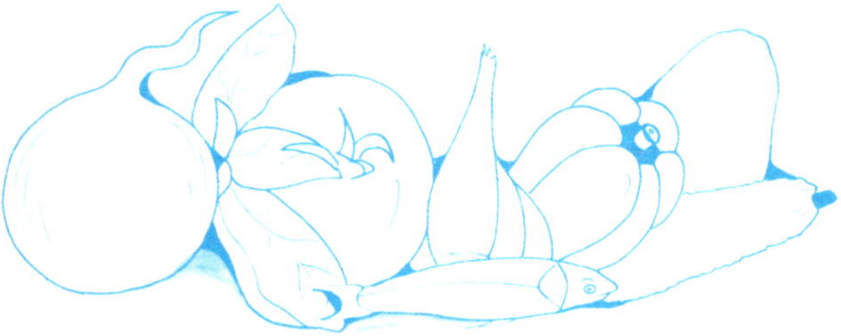

GENOESE GREEN RAVIOLI

RAVIOLI VERDI ALLA GENOVESE

SERVES 4

For the dough:
400 gr. Flour
4 eggs
1 tbsp extra virgin olive oil

For the filling:
300 gr. Minced veal meat
500 gr. spinach
100 gr. butter
Sprigs parsley
Basil leaves
2 onions
2 eggs
bunch of silverbeet
sprigs chervil

Dressing:
Meat sauce
50 gr. Grated parmesan cheese
Salt and pepper

Mix the flour, eggs and oil to obtain a soft dough. Wash and steam spinach and silver beet until tender, drain and chop finely. Finely chop onion and sauté with butter in saucepan, add veal mince and allow to cook until golden brown, add the silverbeet and the spinach, season with salt and pepper. Remove from heat, add finely chopped basil and chervil, eggs and mix well.
Roll out dough into thin sheet, cut out circles and place a level teaspoon of mixture into centre of each circle, fold over to enclose filling and fold into half moons pressing firmly.
To close. Cook ravioli in large saucepan of salted boiling water. When the ravioli begin to rise, drain. Place on serving dish, stir in meat sauce, season with salt and pepper, top with grated parmesan cheese. Mix well an serve.

RISOTTO ALLA MARINARA

SERVES 4 TO 6

400 gr. Rice
200 gr. shelled shrimps
100 gr. baby octopus
Sprigs parsley
Basil leaves
1 hot pepper
200 gr. cleaned clams
100 gr. baby cuttlefish
2 cloves garlic
4 tbsp tomato sauce
4 tbsp extra virgin olive oil
Salt

Clean all fish and cut into pieces. Heat oil in large frying pan, add finely chopped cloves of garlic, basil and parsley, add tomato sauce, the hot pepper and salt. Cover and allow to cook for at least ten minutes. Add fish and continue cookingr. Aside, boil rice until tender, drain. Add rice to fish, stir and sauté for a couple of seconds before servingr.

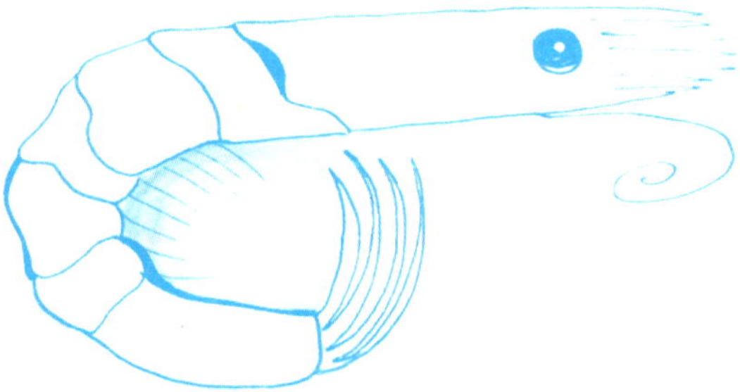

REEF SPAGHETTI
SPAGHETTI ALLO SCOGLIO
SERVES 4

400 gr. Spaghetti
200 gr. Small squid
200 gr. Hard-shelled clams
4 cloves garli
Shredded hot pepper (optional)
1/2 glass extra virgin olive oil
200 gr. shrimps
300 gr. Mussels
200 gr. Dublin bay prawns
sprigs parley
1/2 glass white wine
Salt

Sautè finely chopped clove garlic and a hot pepper in an oiled frying pan. Add a drop of wine, the squid, prawns, parsley and pinch of salt. Cook for at least 15 minutes . Steam open the mussels, then sauté in oil with finely chopped clove garlic and remainder of wine. Add fettuccine to large saucepan of salted boiling water. Boil rapidly, uncovered until pasta is just tender, drain, then sauté in the pan with the baby squid, shrimps and prawns. Pour onto serving dish and garnish with mussels and chopped parsley.

SPAGHETTI WITH TUNA FISH
SPAGHETTI CON IL TONNO

SERVES 4

400 gr. Spaghetti
1 clove garlic
2 salted anchovies
1 can peeled tomatoes
100 gr. tuna fish packed in olive oil
1/2 glass extra virgin olive oil
A pinch of marjoram
Salt and pepper

Heat oil in a saucepan, add clove garlic and remove as soon as it turns golden brown, then add the cleaned filleted anchovies cut into pieces. Allow to cook slowly until melted then add the peeled diced tomatoes. Continue cooking on low heat and when sauce has thickened add the crushed tuna with its oil. Let cook for another couple of minutes, then add a little salt, pepper and marjoram.
Add spaghetti to large saucepan of salted boiling water, boil rapidly, uncovered, until pasta is just tender, drain. Stir in the tuna sauce.

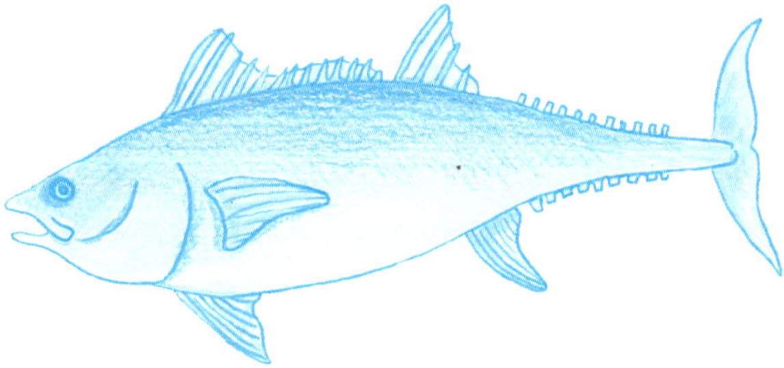

SPAGHETTI WITH CLAMS
SPAGHETTI ALLE VONGOLE

SERVES 4

400 gr. Spaghetti
1 kg. clams
1 clove garlic
1/2 glass dry white wine
Sprigs of parsley
1/2 glass olive oil
Salt and hot pepper (optional)

Wash and scrub clams and let them sit in salted water so they can purge themselves of sand. Wash again under running water. Sautè garlic and the red pepper in oil. When garlic starts to brown, add clams. Stir often and when clams are open add wine. Cook spaghetti in boiling salted water, drain when tender. Combine pasta to pan with clam sauce. Stir constantly over medium heat. Sprinkle with parsley and serve hot.

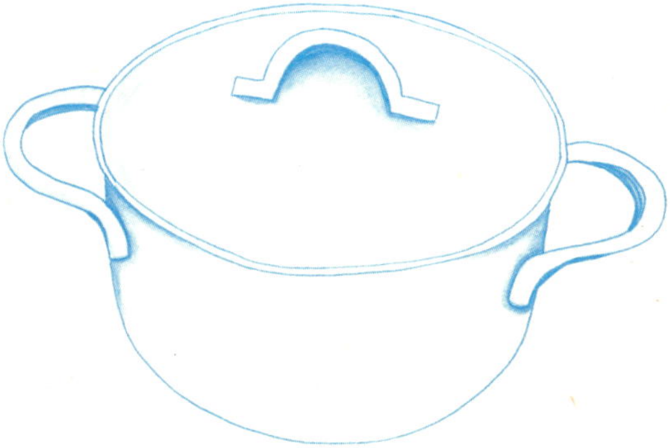

TAGLIOLINI WITH FISH SAUCE CAMOGLI FISHERMEN'S STYLE

TAGLIOLINI DI PESCE ALLA MANIERA DEI PESCATORI DI CAMOGLI

SERVES 4

500 gr. Mixed reef fish
400 gr. Tagliolini pasta
50 gr. Butter
Sprigs parsley
1 glass dry white wine
Lemon rind
1 tbsp flour
Salt and white pepper

Wash and clean fish, fillet, and remove backbone and all small bones. Place in large frying pan with a slab of butter, finely chopped parsley and a small lemon rind, top with dry white wine. Cover and allow to cook for about 15 minutes. Cook fish on both sides. If necessary, add more wine. Add a little flour to thicken sauce, stirring until blended and smooth. Cook the tagliolini in boiling salted water, drain when pasta is ready. Add pasta to the fish sauce, stir gently over medium heat until combined and serve hot.

PASTA IN BASIL SAUCE
TRENETTE AL PESTO

SERVES 4

500 g trenette pasta
1 potato
100 gr. String beans

Basil sauce:
45 basil leaves
2 cloves garlic
Pinch of coarse salt
2 tbsp of grated parmesan cheese
2 tbsp grated ewe's milk cheese
2 tbsp fresh pin nuts
1/2 glass extra virgin olive oil

Combine basil, cloves garlic, coarse salt, pine-nuts and cheese in marble mortar adding oil in thin stream and mash with pestle. Continue mashing until mixture is thick and creamy. In a large saucepan of boiling hot water, add cut string beans and diced potato and the trenette pasta. When pasta is tender, drain. Reserve some cooking liquid. Transfer pasta to serving dish, stir in pesto sauce and , if necessary, add reserved liquid.

TRENETTE IN WALNUT SAUCE
TRENETTE IN SALSA DI NOCE
SERVES 4

400 gr. Trenette pasta
12 walnuts
1/2 litre fresh cream
40 gr. Butter
Salt and pepper

Shell pine nuts, mash the nuts in a mortar and put into a bowl, add the slightly warmed liquid cream. Stir with care. Cook the pasta in boiling salted water until tender, drain. Stir in melted butter and top with nut and cream sauce.

TROFIE DI RECCO
SERVES 4

For dough:
500 gr. durum wheat

Sauce:
2 tbsp extra virgin olive oil
50 gr. Grated parmesan cheese.

Make a mound of flour on work surface. Add a ladle of boiling water . Work and knead until smooth dough is obtained. Break off bits about size of chick-peas and roll under the palm of the hand to create an elongated shape with curling ends. Add two tbsp of oil to abundant boiling salted water and the “trofie”. when trofie rise to surface, drain and serve with pesto sauce and grated parmesan cheese.

MUSSEL SOUP FROM LA SPEZIA GULF

ZUPPA DI MITILI DEL GOLFO DELLA SPEZIA

SERVES 4

2 kg. mussels
Sprigs of parsley
1 clove garlic
1/2 glass extra virgin olive oil
1 glass white wine
1 glass tomato paste
Salt and pepper

Finely cop parsley and garlic and allow to sauté in oil for a couple of minutes. Add cleaned mussels and leave to open. Remove mussels from pan as soon as open. Place in a saucepan with the filtered cooking liquid, wine, salt and pepper, tomato paste and a litre of water. Allow to cook for at least 20 minutes. Serve on toasted bread.

FISH SOUP
ZUPPA DI PESCE
SERVES 4 TO 6

300 gr. Redfish
300 gr. Octopus
1 onion
Sprigs of parsley
4tbsp extra virgin olive oil
300 gr. Reef mullets
300 g mussels
5 cloves garlic
500 gr. Can peeled tomatoes
Salt

Place finely chopped onion and crushed cloves garlic in an oiled deep earthenware pot. Add the peeled tomatoes, chopped parsley and tip of hot pepper, if desired. Allow to cook for about 10 minutes, then add the fish, mussels previously opened by cooking in pan, the cleaned octopus, filleted and stripped of fish-bone. Add salt and serve soup with toasted home-made bread rubbed with garlic.

Second course

Secondi piatti

ANCHOVIES WITH BEETS
ACCIUGHE CON LE BIETOLE

SERVES 4

A big bunch of wide stalk beets
16 salted anchovies
2-3 cloves garlic
1/2 glass extra virgin olive oil
Salt and white pepper.

Carefully wash and cut up beets and boil for 10 minutes in salted water, drain till all water is removed. Wash anchovies well, remove back-bone and divide into two. Heat oil in pan, sauté the greens with two cloves garlic for about 10 minutes, remove cloves garlic and add the anchovies. Stir well, season with pepper and cook another ten minutes.

GENOESE STYLE ROAST
ARROSTO ALLA GENOVESE

SERVES 4

1 kg. veal rumpsteak (in a single piece)
6 onions
4 tbsp flour
Salt
2 glasses stock
1/2 glass dry white wine
4 tbsp extra virgin olive oil

Dust meat lightly with flour, shake off excess flour. Heat oil in pan, add the meat with sliced onions. Cook until onion soften. Salt and add stock, cook for two hours, stir frequently. After two hours, allow to cool and slice. To prepare roast sauce sieve the onion sauce into a saucepan, add white wine and flour. Allow to cook for a couple of minutes taking care that no lumps form. Pour over roast and heat up a couple of minutes before servingr.

ROAST BEEF FILLET
ARROSTO DI FILLETTO DI BUE

Serves 4

800 gr. Beef fillet
1/2 glass white wine
1/2 extra virgin olive oil
Sprig rosemary
Salt and pepper
1 onion
30 gr. butter
Bay leaf
2 cloves

Melt butter in a saucepan, add the fillet, oil, chopped onion, salt and pepper. Cook roast, turn on all sides, add white wine, bay leaf, sprig of rosemary and cloves. Cook on low heat, covered, for at least 2 hours, turning the roast at intervals. Serve hot, slicing on the spot.

CALF ENTRAILS 5 TERRE STYLE
AXELLE (BUDELLINE) ALL'USO DELLE 5 TERRE

Serves 4

1 kgr.. of calf entrails
1/2 glass extra virgin olive oil
1 glass wine vinegar
Salt and pepper

Wash the entrails thoroughly in water and vinegar, turn inside out and remove any excess lumps of fat. Cook on grill or in pan with very little oil. Once grilled, serve with crude oil, salt and freshly ground black pepper.

SALTED COD IN THE GREEN
BACCALÀ AL VERDE

Serves 4

1 kg. softened salted cod
1 litre milk

50 gr. Flour
1 onion
1 carrot
1 celery stick
2 cloves garlic
Sprigs parsley
5 anchovy fillets
20 gr. Dried mushrooms softened in water
1 tbsp salted capers
1 tbsp pine nuts
1 glass dry white wine
400 gr. potatoes
8 tbsp extra virgin olive oil
salt

Rinse excess salt from cod then soak cod, at least a day beforehand, in cold water. Change water several times. Drain cod, cut into serving pieces, and place in bowl with milk for a couple of hours. Heat large saucepan with 4 tbsp olive oil, sauté the chopped celery stick, onion, carrot , cloves garlic, parsley and mashed anchovy fillets. Process washed capers, the pine-nuts and sliced mushrooms; dilute mixture with white wine, stir and then add to vegetables and allow to cook on medium heat for another 10 minutes. Add cod pieces, tossed in flour. Season with salt and continue cooking for another 20 minutes. Boil potatoes, drain, peel and slice thinly. Add 2 tbsp oil to oven pan, spread a layer of potatoes, add thin stream oil and salt. Spread cod pieces on potatoes, add the cooking sauce and place in hot oven 180°C and allow to turn golden brown. Serve hot.

BURIDDA DI SEPPIE

SERVES 4

1/2 kg. Cuttlefish
6 ripe tomatoes
400 gr. fresh shelled peas
1 onion
Sprigs of parsley
1 tbsp salted capers
1 glass dry white wine
1/2 glass extra virgin olive oil
Salt and pepper

Clean cuttlefish, remove cuttle bone, eyes and black ink sac, wash and cut into strips and sauté in earthenware pan with washed capers, oil, chopped onion and garlic. When golden brown, add tomatoes, pour glass of wine, season with salt and pepper, cover and let cook for at least an hour on low heat. If necessary, add ladle of stock. When almost done, add shelled peas and continue cookingr. Before serving the "buridda" sprinkle with finely chopped parsley.

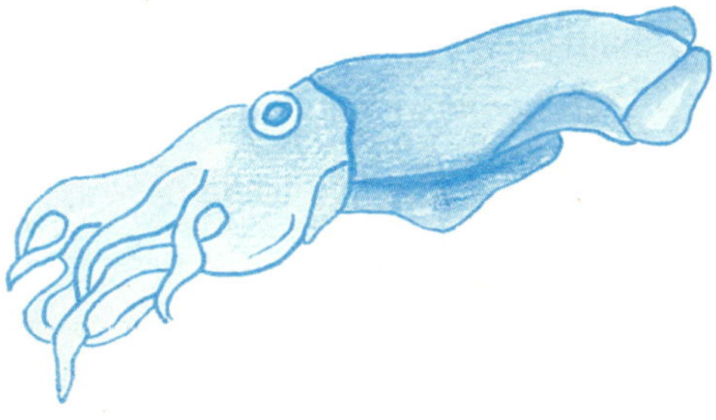

BURRIDDA LIGURE

SERVES 6

200 gr. Eel
200 gr. Congers
200 gr. Cuttlefish
1 celery stick
2 cloves garlic
Sprigs parsley
5 small ripe tomatoes
1 tbsp flour
Salt and pepper
200 gr. blenny fish
200 gr. Octopus
200 gr. Red fish
1 onion
2 salted anchovies
40 gr. dried mushrooms
1/2 glass extra virgin olive oil
6 slices toasted home-made bread

Clean and remove back-bone for fish, cut into pieces. Heat oil in earthenware pan and sauté finely chopped onion, celery stick and carrot. Place fish on the vegetable mixture and add diced tomatoes. Season with salt and pepper, cover and allow to cook for a quarter of an hour. After having washed and drained mushrooms previously put in water, add to soup. Add a glass of hot water and continue cooking for another ten minutes. Serve the buridda hot over slices of toasted bread, sprinkled with chopped parsley.

CAPPON MAGRO

SERVES 4 TO 6

Fish:

Gurnard fish
24 king prawns
1 small lobster
10 slices of dried dolphin fillets

Vegetables:

1 small cauliflower
4 carrots
1 celery stalk
200 gr. string beans
4 artichokes
1 bunch bitter roots

Sauce:

Clove garlic
Sprigs parsley
25 gr. Pine nuts
25 gr. capers
3-4 pickled cucumbers
8-10 baby mushrooms in oil
Sea biscuits
6-7 pitted black olives
1 small bread roll
1 glass wine vinegar
2 hard boiled egg yolks
2 fresh egg yolks
1/2 glass extra virgin olive oil
salt

Boil the gurnard, remove skin and bones, fillet and cut into pieces. Boil the lobster and prawns, shell and cut meat into strips. Dress fish with oil, lemon and pinch of salt. Cook vegetables whole and separately in abundant salted water, drain and cut into small pieces, dress with oil, vinegar and salt and, keep separate. Process garlic, parsley, pine-nuts, cucumbers, capers, baby mushrooms and bread previously softened in vinegar and well drained, egg yolks, salt and pepper. Add oil and vinegar and mix well to get a fluid consistency.
Dip the sea biscuits in a water and vinegar mixture to soften them. Take a large serving dish and prepare a layer of sea-biscuits, add a layer of slices of dried dolphin fillets, spread a tbsp of the sauce, a layer of vegetables, a little sauce, the fish and top with the remaining sauce. Garnish with prawns and serve.

GENOESE STUFFED VEAL FLANK

CIMA ALLA GENOVESE

SERVES 4 TO 6

800 gr. Veal breast
150 gr. veal flesh
50 gr. sweetbread
1 veal testicle
100 gr. veal spine marrow
20 gr. Pine – nuts
Sprig marjoram
2 onions
2 litres stock
1/2 glass extra virgin olive oil
1 can spring peas
1 glass dry white wine
8 eggs
100 gr. grated parmesan cheese
1 clove garlic

Sew the paunch of veal with cotton thread to form a rectangular shape and leaving one side open. Fill with water to check that there are no leaks, empty and allow to drip. Heat a little oil in a casserole (earthenware , if possible) add sliced onion, veal flesh, cubed sweetbread and veal testicle. When ingredients are browned, pour a glass of dry white wine. Half cook the brain and bone marrow, drain and peel off skin, cut into cubes and place in a bowl. When all wine in casserole has evaporated, remove the meats and put with the other ingredients in the bow. Add the beaten eggs, grated parmesan cheese, the peas, the pine-nuts and the finely chopped marjoram and garlic. Add salt and combine. Spoon the mixture into the paunch and sew the last opened part. Fill a pot with cold water, add carrot, celery stalk and onion. When the broth is warm add the stuffed paunch of veal and let it cook for 2 hours. When cooked , remove and place between two dishes with a weight on top to drain any excess liquid. Serve cold and thinly sliced.

RABBIT COOKED IN ROSSESE DI DOLCEACQUA

CONIGLIO AL ROSSESE DI DOLCEACQUA

SERVES 4

1 rabbit
onion
Celery stalk
50 gr. pine-nuts
50 gr. walnut kernels
Sprig rosemary
Thyme
Bay leaves
1 glass of Rossese di dolceacqua wine
1/2 glass extra virgin olive oil
Salt

Wash and cut rabbit into pieces, put aside head and liver. Place pieces in pan with oil, bay leaves, rosemary and thyme and allow to cook until meat is browned on all sides. Aside boil rabbit head and liver in salted water. Blend onion, celery stalk, pine nuts and walnut kernels. Add this mixture to the rabbit, continually adding stock obtained from rabbit head and liver. Add wine and allow to evaporate slowly. When sauce has thickened add salt and pepper and serve.

LAMB CHOPS LIGURIAN STYLE
COSTOLETTE D'AGNELLO ALLA LIGURE

SERVES 4

16 lamb chops
Sprigs parsley
Breadcrumbs
1 lemon
Salt and pepper
1/2 glass extra virgin olive oil
1 egg
4 artichokes
Clove garlic

Clean artichokes, peeling stalks and stripping away tough outer leaves. Blanch thoroughly in water and lemon juice. Beat egg, season and add finely chopped garlic and parsley. Dip the lamb chops in the mixture and toss in breadcrumbs. Deep fry, drain on absorbent paper. Serve on dish with a spread of thinly cut raw artichokes with salt and oil dressingr.

FRIED MEAT MIX
FRITTO MISTO DI CARNE

SERVES 4

4 veal steaks
200 gr. veal spinal marrow
4 slices liver
50 gr. grated parmesan cheese
1 cup breadcrumbs
Salt and pepper
4 mince meatballs
Calf brain
4 pieces of sausage
3 eggs
1 glass extra virgin olive oil

Slice all the meats. First dip in 2 beaten eggs and then dip in breadcrumbs. Add last egg to the minced meat, parmesan cheese, salt and pepper. Shape into meat balls and dip in breadcrumbs. Heat oil in large frying pan and fry. Aside, lightly dust liver in flour. Cook liver and sausage in pan. Drain all meats on absorbent paper and serve hot with mixed salad as side dish.

MIXED FISH FRY
FRITTO MISTO DI PESCE
SERVES 4

100 gr. Red mullets
100 gr. anchovies
100 gr. baby cod
100 gr. baby flatfish
Flour
Oil for deep fry

Wash, remove and discard entrails, clean and pat the fish dry. Dip fish in flour until it is well coated Shake off excess flour. Deep fry the fish in hot oil until golden brown. Drain on absorbent paper.

MUSSELS À LA MARINARA
MUSCOLI ALLA MARINARA
SERVES 4

2 kg. mussels
2 cloves garlic
Sprigs parsley
1 glass white wine
Red hot pepper
1/2 glass extra virgin olive oil
Salt and pepper

Scrub mussels and remove beards. Finely chop parsley, garlic cloves and red hot pepper. Heat oil in large pan, add mussels and allow to cook for a couple of minutes. Add glass of white wine. As soon as shells are opened, sprinkle with parsley mixture. Allow to cook another 4-5 minutes. Before removing from heat, season with salt and pepper.

HAKE SAVONA STYLE
NASELLO ALLA SAVONESE
SERVES 4

8 hake fillets
1/2 glass extra virgin olive oil
2 anchovy fillets under oil
4 tbsp carton cream
Salt and pepper
4 tbsp flour
50 gr. Butter
Salted capers
Dash of rum

Carefully wash and dry the hake fillets, salt and toss in flour. Heat butter and oil in pan, add hake fillets and allow to cook for approximately 3 minutes. Turn fillets, add rum to
Flambé then add carton cream. Chop capers and anchovy fillets and add to fish. Cook another couple of minutes, add finely chopped parsley and cloves garlic and serve.

GRILLED ANGLER FISH
PESCATRICE AI FERRI
SERVES 4

1 angler fish of approx.1 1/2 kg.
Sprigs parsley finely chopped
Thyme
Lemon juice
Salt and pepper
Onion
Bay leaf
Marjoram
1/2 glass extra virgin olive oil

Clean fish, removing head, gill, discard entrails and skin. Fillet fish. Place angler fish in deep dish, cover with thinly sliced onion, finely chopped herb mixture of parsley, bay leaf, thyme, marjoram. Add salt and pepper, lemon juice, 2 tbsp of olive oil and allow to marinate at room temperature for 2 hours. Remove fish from marinade. Grill or better still barbecue the fish for about 8-10 minutes on each side, then serve.

SWORDFISH WITH PINE-NUTS, OLIVES AND CAPERS

PESCE SPADA CON PINOLI, OLIVE E CAPPERI

SERVES 4

1 kg. swordfish cut into 4 slices
8 tbsp extra virgin olive oil
1 glass white wine
2 cloves garlic
20 gr. pine nuts
10 gr. capers
2 pinches of oregano
30 brined black olives
Salt and pepper

Toast pine nuts in oven; wash capers under cold running water. Heat oil in large frying pan add chopped cloves garlic. Remove skin from slices of swordfish and place in pan. Sauté and cook fish on each side. Pour in white wine, add the toasted pine nuts, capers, finely chopped parsley and the black olives. Season with salt and pepper. Continue cooking until fish is tender. Serve slices hot, top with the sauce.

CHICKEN GENOESE STYLE
POLLO ALLA GENOVESE

SERVES 4

A chicken
1/2 glass extra virgin olive oil
3 cloves garlic
1 tbsp flour
2 tbsp white vinegar
Rosemary
5-6 sage leaves
Bay leaves
1 lemon
1 glass Vermentino wine
Salt and pepper

Clean the chicken and place in a pot with salted boiling water. Allow to cook for an hour. Heat a little oil in frying pan, sauté crushed cloves garlic, add tbsp flour, vinegar and a ladle of chicken stock. Simmer until sauce is thickened. Salt and add finely chopped herb mixture. Pour the wine and lemon juice onto the sauce and continue cooking for another 15 minutes. Remove chicken from pot and cut into joints. Skim sauce , pour over chicken and serve.

OCTOPUS CASSEROLE
POLPO IN CASSERUOLA
SERVES 4

1 big octopus
5-6 onions
A glass of extra virgin olive oil
4 glass of strong dry red wine
7-8 tomatoes
5-6 potatoes
Salt and pepper

Carefully clean the octopus, cut into big pieces and put in casserole without oil. Allow to roast. Remove when turns dark red. Slice onions and sauté in oil, add diced tomatoes and potatoes, season with salt and pepper. Allow to cook for half an hour, ad octopus, cover with red wine and let cook for three hours on very low heat. Serve with boiled potatoes and toasted bread.

CUTTLEFISH AND POTATOES IN WHITE WINE

SEPPIE E PATATE AL VINO BIANCO

SERVES 4

500 gr. Cuttlefish
500 gr. Potatoes
2 tomatoes
1 onion
Clove garlic
1 glass dry white wine
1/2 glass extra virgin olive oil
Thyme
1 glass vegetable stock
Salt and pepper

Clean cuttlefish. Remove tentacles. Cut tentacles into pieces. Clean and chop onion and clove garlic. Sauté in little oil. Add the cut tentacles. Pour wine and add diced tomatoes, potatoes and the cuttlefish previously cut into strips. Pour a couple of ladles of hot stock and add salt. Cover and cook a further twenty minutes or until cuttlefish is tender. Before serving sprinkle with chopped thyme and pepper.

FLATFISH GENOVESE STYLE
SOGLIOLE ALLA GENOVESE

SERVES 4

4 big flatfish
20-30 basil leaves
2 lemons
100 gr. Pine nuts
8 tbsp flour
1/2 glass extra virgin olive oil
1 cup breadcrumbs
50 gr. butter
Salt and pepper

Wash, clean flatfish (frozen flatfish can also be used, but not ready to use fillets). Dip fish into flour, shake away any excess flour and half-fry in hot oil. Drain and place fried fish on work surface. Remove spine by cutting through centre of fish without removing head or tail. Blend basil leaves, pine-nuts, breadcrumbs, salt and pepper. Spoon mixture into the cavity of the flatfish, season with salt and pepper. Place fish in ovenproof dish, pour lemon juice and melted butter. Bake in oven. Before serving garnish the serving dish with pine-nuts and basil leaves.

STOCKFISH GENOVESE STYLE
STOCCAFISSO ALLA GENOVESE

Serves 4

800 gr. Softened stockfish
500 gr. potatoes
2 salted anchovies
1 glass extra virgin olive oil
1 onion
300 gr. can peeled tomatoes
sprigs parsley
celery stalk
1 glass white wine
salt and pepper
1 carrot
20 gr. pine-nuts

Place stockfish in salted boiling water for a couple of minutes to facilitate removal of skin and bones. Peel and dice potatoes. Finely chop clove garlic, celery stalk, carrot and onions. Finely chop parsley. Sauté the chopped vegetables in casserole in abundant oil for a couple of minutes. Add the stockfish, potatoes, pine nuts and tomatoes. Allow to cook on low heat for at least fifty minutes, frequently adding a tbsp of water and the white wine. Continue cooking until potatoes are tender. Serve after seasoning with salt and pepper.

STOCKFISH À LA MARINARA
STOCCAFISSO ALLA MARINARA

SERVES 4

800 gr. Softened stockfish
6 salted anchovies
20 gr. Pine-nuts
2 cloves garlic
1/2 glass dry white wine
1/2 glass extra virgin olive oil
Salt and pepper

Place the stockfish in salted boiling water for a couple of minutes to facilitate the removal of skin and bones. Wash the anchovies under running water to remove all the salt and remove all bones. Heat oil in deep saucepan, add the anchovies and sliced cloves and a little pepper. Add stockfish cut into pieces and the pine-nuts. Allow to cook for at least 40 minutes, adding white wine. Stir gently.

FISH PLATTER
TEGLIA DI PESCE
SERVES 4

500 gr. Fish fillets
2 tbsp chopped fresh basil leaves
50 gr. Fresh baby mushrooms
4 tbsp extra virgin olive oil
3 shallots
50 gr. butter
1 glass dry white wine
salt and pepper
8 cloves garlic
2 dl. Fresh cream
4 tomatoes

Peel, remove seeds and dice tomatoes. Heat oil in saucepan, add 2 peeled cloves garlic. Cook over medium heat for 5 minutes and then add salt. Finely chop shallots and spread them onto a greased baking dish. Spread a layer of thinly cut and washed baby mushrooms. Pour wine and then spread fish fillets. Season with salt and pepper and bake in moderate oven (180°C) for 25 minutes.
Aside, process remaining cloves garlic, cream, salt and ground pepper. Cook over low heat without boilingr. Remove fish dish from oven, stir in the hot tomatoes and basil. Serve with the garlic and cream sauce.

MEAT ROLLS
TOMAXELLE
SERVES 4

8 slices of veal loin
100 gr. Lean mince meat
100 gr. Sweetbreads
50 gr. Calf brain
3 eggs
Flour
1/2 glass extra virgin olive oil
Ladle meat broth
Salt
fresh breadcrumbs
grated parmesan cheese
1 onion
1/2 glass milk
pinch of mixed spices (cinnamon, cloves, pepper, nutmeg, hot peppers)
1 glass dry white wine

Heat oil in saucepan, add onion cut into pieces and the meats. Sauté and pour half a glass of dry white wine. Allow to evaporate. Sieve and place in bowl, add the eggs, grated parmesan cheese, fresh breadcrumbs moistened in milk and a pinch of the mixed spices, season with salt and mix well. Lightly pound the veal slices. Spoon mixture onto each veal slice and roll, sew with white thread. Dip in flour and cook in little oil. When golden brown, sprinkle with remaining wine, leave to evaporate and continue cooking, adding hot stock to avoid becoming too dry.

TUNA IMPERIA STYLE
TONNO ALLA IMPERIESE

SERVES 4

4 thick slices fresh tuna fish
100 gr. Flour
1/2 glass extra virgin olive oil
Sprigs parsley
1 onion
bay leaf
1 tbsp salted capers
A pinch of cinnamon
1/2 glass dry white wine
Salt and freshly ground pepper

Chop onion and parsley finely and sauté a couple of minutes in frying pan. Dust tuna slices with flour and add fish to the frying pan. Fry until both sides are golden brown, season with salt and pepper, sprinkle with white wine. Allow to evaporate a little, add capers, crumbled bay leaf and a little cinnamon. Cover, allow to cook over medium heat for at least 20 minutes adding a little water when required. Serve tuna with its sauce.

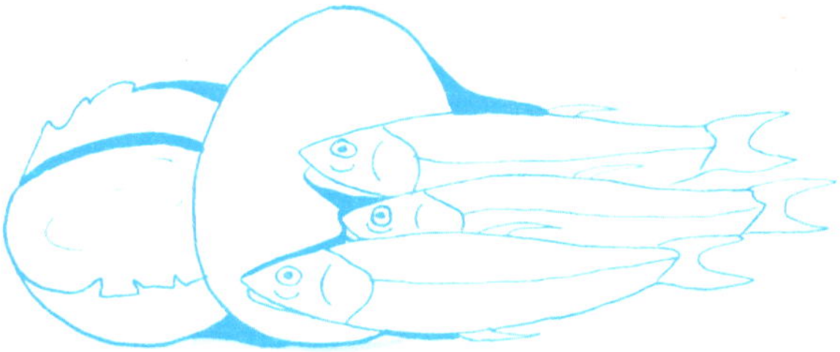

STUFFED SQUID
TOTANI RIPIENI
SERVES 4

800 gr. Squid
200 gr. baked ham
Sprigs of parsley
1 onion
Fresh breadcrumbs
1/2 glass milk
4-5 sage leaves
sprig rosemary
fresh hot pepper
4 tbsp brandy
1 glass white wine
2 eggs
1/2 glass extra virgin olive oil
salt and pepper

Clean squid; remove body beak, discard eyes an entrails. Wash and pat dry after having cut tentacles. Add tentacles and hoods to pan, top with cold water spiced with a slice of onion. Allow to boil on medium heat. After 20 minutes, remove hoods and continue cooking the tentacles for another 20 minutes, drain and let cool. Process ham, squid tentacles, the bread softened in milk and then squeezed to remove excess liquid, and whisk all with eggs, add salt, pepper and chopped parsley. Spoon mixture into squid hoods. Heat little oil in large pan, add chopped sage leaves, rosemary and hot pepper (optional), a sliced onion, and clove garlic. Place the stuffed squids onto this mixture, sprinkle brandy over squid and allow to cook, adding white wine, for 40-50 minutes. Season before servingr.

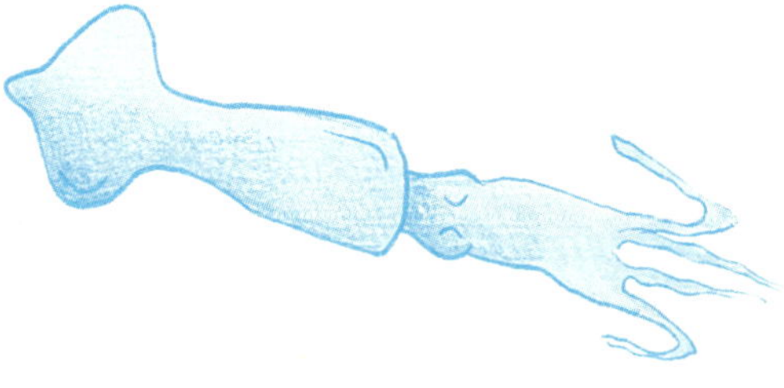

RED MULLETS OF THE CINQUE TERRE

TRIGLIE DELLE CINQUE TERRE

Serves 4

1 kg. Red mullets
500 gr. ripe tomatoes
3 cloves garlic
1 celery stalk
2 tbsp tomato paste
Sprigs parsley
1/2 glass extra virgin olive oil
Salt and pepper

Chop the parsley, and separately the clove garlic an celery stalk. Heat 2 tbsp of oil in saucepan, add half of the chopped parsley, clove garlic and celery stalk and sauté on low heat. Add the peeled, seedless and coarsely cut tomatoes, the tomato paste, salt and pepper. Cook for at least 15 minutes. Strain the sauce in fine sieve. Clean red mullets, gut, wash, pat dry and fry in abundant oil. Transfer a couple of tb-sp of the frying oil to an oval saucepan (preferably earthenware) place the fried fish in single layer and cover with the sauce. Allow to cook for 5 minutes, then serve, sprinkled with chopped parsley.

TRIPE GENOVESE STYLE
TRIPPA ALLA GENOVESE

SERVES 4

300 gr. mixed tripe
1 can peeled tomatoes
1 medium onion
1 celery stalk
2 carrots
2-3 cloves garlic
1 glass red wine
1/2 glass extra virgin olive oil
100 gr sheep's milk cheese
thyme
rosemary
salt and black pepper

Finely chop cloves garlic, celery stalk, carrot, onion, rosemary and thyme. Place in pot, preferably earthenware, with oil an sauté. When the vegetables are golden brown, add the thinly sliced tripe. Allow to cook for half an hour, add wine and continue cooking on medium to high heat until evaporated. Crush tomatoes and add to tripe. Cover and cook on low heat for a couple of hours, stir when necessary. Serve tripe in soup plate, with ground black pepper and a sprinkle of grated sheep's milk cheese. Cover with a stream of olive oil.

ROAST VEAL WITH OLIVES AND PINE-NUTS

VITELLO CON OLIVE E PINOLI

SERVES 4

800 gr. Roast veal
2 anchovies in brine
80 gr. Green stoned olives
50 gr. Pine-nuts
1 tbsp salted capers
300 gr. dry wild mushrooms
1 glass dry white wine
2 cloves garlic
30 gr. butter
1/2 glass extra virgin olive oil
salt and pepper

Soften the mushrooms in warm water, drain well and chop finely . Place roast in a suitable sized pan, add butter, 3 tbsp of oil and a sliced clove of garlic. Cook on all sides, pour wine and allow to slowly evaporate, season with salt and pepper. Cover and bake in oven preheated to 180°C for at least an hour: Sprinkle with water or hot broth, if required. Aside, wash , fillet, and cut anchovies into pieces. Wash and chop
Capers. Heat oil in a small saucepan, add anchovies, pin-nuts, chopped olives, capers and mushrooms. Allow to cook on low heat, stir and cook for at least 15 minutes: remove clove garlic, season with salt and pepper. When roast is cooked remove for the pan and add the olive sauce to the roast sauce. Cook a couple of minutes. Spread over the sliced roast.

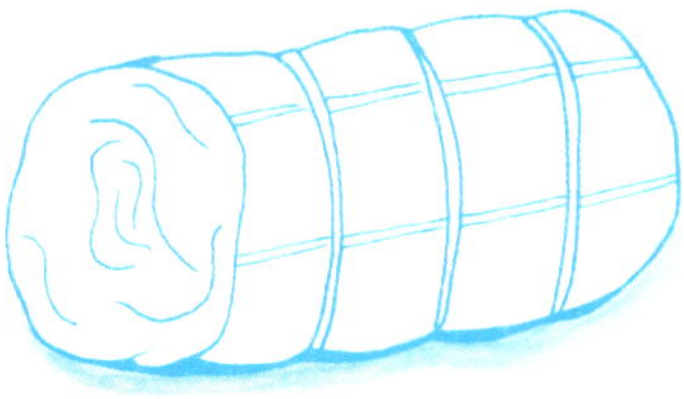

Side dishes

Contorni

OVEN-BAKED ARTICHOKES
CARCIOFI AL FORNO
SERVES 4

8 artichokes
1/2 glass extravirgin olive oil
Salt and pepper

Wash the artichokes, peel stalks and strip away tough outer leaves, keeping the tender part of the artichoke. Stand artichokes in an oiled oven tray. Slightly open the leaves and sprinkle with oil, season with salt and pepper. Bake in oven at 150°C for 40 minutes. Baking time depends on artichoke size so make sure artichokes are baked before servingr.

ARTICHOKE IN BASIL SAUCE
CARCIOFI AL PESTO
SERVES 4

8 artichokes
Jar of basil sauce
Basil leaves
Salt

Wash the artichokes, strip away tough outer leaves and thorns, leave tender part. Cook in slightly salted boiling water. Drain, split them in half and arrange on serving platter. Add a tbsp of basil sauce on each half and garnish platter with basil leaves.

LIGURIAN STYLE CARDOONS
CARDI ALLA LIGURE

SERVES 4

1 kg. cardoons
50 gr. butter
Béchamel sauce
A lemon
80 gr. grated parmesan cheese
Salt and pepper

Wash cardoons, remove tougher outer parts, cut into 5 cm. long pieces and put in water mixed with lemon juice. Melt a little butter in a saucepan and add the cardoons, season with salt and pepper, cover. When cardoons are cooked transfer to a greased baking dish, cover with béchamel sauce and combine. Sprinkle abundant grated parmesan cheese and bake in pre-heated oven at 220°C for 15 minutes until golden brown. Serve very hot without removing for baking dish.

GENOVESE STYLE STRING BEANS
FAGIOLINI ALLA GENOVESE
SERVES 4

500 gr. string beans
Sprigs of parsley
Clove garlic
4 salted anchovies
4 tbsp extra virgin olive oil
Salt and pepper

Wash anchovies under running water, remove salt and backbone. Clean, wash, trim tips and boil string beans in salted water. Drain and set aside. Heat oil in frying pan, sauté finely chopped clove of garlic and parsley, add the anchovies, stir constantly until dissolved. Add string beans and combine, cook another couple of minutes. Serve hot, season with salt and pepper.

SAUTÉED MUSHROOMS
FUNGHI AL FUNGHETTO
SERVES 4

600 gr. mixed wild mushrooms
2 cloves garlic
1/2 glass extra virgin olive oil
2 pinches of oregano
Salt

Carefully clean mushrooms, remove dirt and slice. Heat large quantity of oil in frying pan with 2 cloves garlic, add mushrooms. Cook on low heat. When cloves garlic golden brown, remove. Add oregano and salt, continue cooking on low heat for 15 minutes.

SALAD VENTIMIGLIA STYLE
INSALATA DI VENTIMIGLIA

SERVES 4

2 ripe tomatoes
2 sweet bell peppers
1 cucumber
10 radishes
1 sweet red onion
400 gr. fresh shelled broadbeans
basil leaves
1/2 glass extra virgin olive oil
1 celery stalk
3 tbsp vinegar
20 stoned oven-baked black olives
2 cloves garlic
3 hard boiled eggs
10 unsalted anchovy fillets
250 gr. undercut of tuna fish
5 wedge cut artichokes
10 big green olives
salt

Wash and slice vegetables, place in large salad bowl. The crushed cloves of garlic can be left or otherwise removed from the bowl, according to taste. Add the crumbled tuna undercut, the sliced hard-boiled eggs and the coarsely cut unsalted anchovy fillets. Aside prepare the dressingr. In a small bowl, mix oil, water and salt, and torn basil leaves. Pour over salad and toss well before servingr.

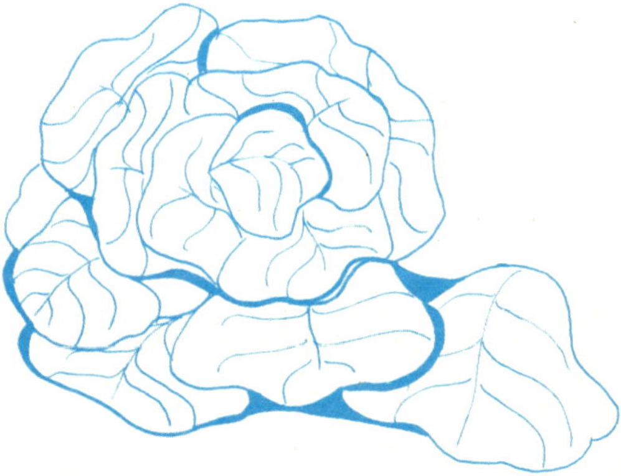

BAKING DISH OF POTATOES

PATATE NELLA TEGLIA

SERVES 4

1 kg. of potatoes
1 onion
200 gr. grated ewe's milk cheese
50 gr. butter
Sprigs of parsley
Salt and pepper
3 tbsp flour
1/2 litre milk
1/2 glass extra virgin olive oil
250 gr. tuma (cheese from Valle Argentina)

Peel and thinly slice potatoes. In a tureen, add 3 tbsp of flour, a 1/2 litre milk, 250gr. Shredded tuma cheese, half of the grated ewe's milk cheese, part of the sliced onion and 2 tbsp of oil . Add the potatoes and stir. Oil an oven tray (the "foglia" is used in the Valle Argentina) and pour the ingredients, spread evenly and cover with remaining grated cheese and slabs of butter. Bake in oven at 150°C for at least an hour, cover with aluminium foil.

VEGETABLE MARROW GENOVESE STYLE

ZUCCHINE TRIFOLATE ALLA GENOVESE

SERVES 4

600 gr. Vegetable marrow
2 cloves garlic
40-50 basil leaves
4 tbsp extra vergin olive oil
Sprigs parsley
Salt and pepper

Wash vegetable marrows and dice. Heat oil in pan with two cloves garlic. Add diced marrows and cook on medium heat for at least 10 minutes or until golden brown. Add salt. Stir occasionally. Cooking completed, add parsley and basil leaves and stir delicately. Serve hot.

Desserts
Dolci

GAVENOLA ALMOND COOKIES
AMARETTI DI GAVENOLA

SERVES 4

250 gr. sugar
50 gr. armelline
20 gr. butter
2 egg whites
100 gr. sweet almonds
50 gr. flour

Peel and toast the almonds and "armelline" in oven for a couple of minutes. Finely chop in processor. Beat egg whites with sugar till stiffened, add almonds and armelline gently stirring until mixture is firm. If mixture is too stiff, beat in another egg white; on contrary, if mixture too soft add more sugar. Shape into small balls, the size of walnuts and place on a greased oven pan sprinkled with flour. Leave space between the biscuits because increase in size. Preheat oven to 150°C and bake 10-12 minutes.

ANISEED BISCUITS
ANICINI

SERVES 4

500 gr. sugar
1 small glass orange scented water
400 gr. flour
10 eggs
1 tbsp aniseeds
Butter

Break eggs, separate yolks from whites. Beat yolks with sugar in large bowl. Apart beat egg whites until stiff, add yolk and sugar mixture, the aniseeds, the orange-scented water. Continue stirring gently and fold in flour. Stir gently and allow to rest for 10 minutes. Butter a 10cm baking tin and spread the mixture evenly onto it. Pre-heat the oven to 180°C and bake for about 10 minutes. Stand to cool. Cut into 2cm thick slices, Place on rack and return to oven. Bake for a further 5 minutes until biscuits turn crispy. Serve the aniseed biscuits cold.

LAGACCIO BISCUITS
BISCOTTI DI LAGACCIO

SERVES 4

600 gr. flour
100 gr. butter
200 gr. sugar
100 gr. fennel seeds
1 glass milk

Mix all the ingredients in a bowl into dough and stand for a couple of hours covered with tea-towel. Turn dough out onto work surface and shape into long rolls. Make diagonal cuts along the rolls 3cm apart. Pre-heat oven to 150°C and bake until firm. Remove from oven and give a definite cut along the diagonal cuts and again place in oven to complete bakingr.

BRUGNATO BISCUITS
CANESTRELLI DI BRUGNATO

SERVES 4

500 gr. flour
2 eggs
400 gr. butter
4tbsp honey
200 gr. sugar
1 tbsp aniseeds
Yeast

On a work surface add melted butter to flour, sugar and 2 yolks, add the chopped anise seeds and honey. Knead and roll out evenly to a 1 1/2 cm. thickness. Cut out biscuits with cutter, brush them lightly with egg white. Place on slightly greased baking pan and bake in oven at 180°C for 20 minutes.

CHESTNUT CRUST
CASTAGNACCIO

SERVES 4

300 gr. chestnut flour
2 tbsp extra virgin olive oil
30 gr. pine-nuts
50 gr. sugar
A pinch of salt
250 gr. milk
50 gr. orange zest
50 gr. raisins
30 gr. butter

Place raisins in bowl with warm water to soften. In a bow, add the chestnut flour, then gradually add salt, sugar, olive oil and milk. Stir with wooden spoon. Dilute mixture by adding a little water to obtain a liquid batter. Add drained raisins, orange zest, pine-nuts and chopped walnuts. Stir in all the ingredients. Grease and sprinkle flour on a baking pan an spread out the mixture. Dribble on a little olive oil and small slabs of butter. Pre-heat oven to 180°C and bake for an hour.

CHIAVARI CAKE
CIAVAI

SERVES 4

A sponge cake
1 l of cream
6 almond cookies
30 gr. sugar
20 gr. icing sugar
A small glass of Cucaçao liqueur
A small glass of rum
3 eggs (only yolks)
1/2 glass Marsala wine
30 gr. butter
25-30 lingue di gatto (similar to ladyfinger biscuits only thinner)

Split a sponge cake in half. Brush the lower half with a mixture of rum and Curaçao liqueur and top with a layer of whipped cream. Aside, prepare egg flip by beating egg yolks with 30gr sugar and Marsala wine until creamy. Spread over the whipped cream and then spread another layer of whipped cream. Brush the other half of the cake with Cucaçao liqueur and join together with other half cake. Spread top o cake with whipped cream and ladyfinger biscuits. Keep in fridge before servingr.

ST. JOSEPH'S FRITTERS
FRITELLE DI SAN GIUSEPPE

SERVES 4

500 gr. flour
100 gr. sugar
200 gr. raisins – soaked and drained
3 eggs
2 glasses milk
20 gr. baker's yeast
1/2 glass extra virgin olive oil
Icing sugar
A pinch of salt

Separate yolk from egg whites. Fold flour and 1 glass of mi8lk in a bowl. Warm other glass of milk and use to dissolve the baker's yeast and then add to the flour. Add yolks, salt and the raisins. Stir until combined and when mixture is smooth, cover and set aside for an hour or until size has doubled. Whisk egg whites and lightly fold into mixture. Drop heaped spoonsful of mixture into boiling oil. Drain excess oil on absorbent paper. Sprinkle with icing sugar.

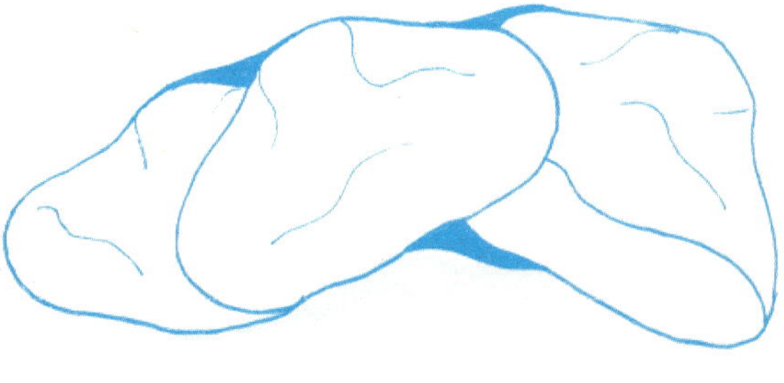

COOKIES FROM SAVONA
GOBELETTI DI SAVONA
SERVES 4

400 gr. flour
250 .r sugar
1 egg
150 gr. butter
1 tbsp Marsala wine
Apricot jam
1/2 glass milk

Sift flour onto work surface, add sugar, egg, softened butter, milk and Marsala wine. Mix together and let stand for an hour. Roll out dough and cut into round with cutter an top with apricot jam and cover with another round of dough. Pre-heat oven to 180°C and bake for 15 minutes.

PACIUGO
SERVES 4

1/2 litre whipped cream
4 tbsp of chocolate ice-cream
8 tbsp o fruit flavoured ice-cream (at pleasure)
1 peach
2 apricots
1 banana
4 tbsp black cherries in syrup
4 tbsp raspberry syrup

Pour frozen cream in a long glass then add a spoon of chocolate ice-cream, a couple of spoonsful of fruit flavoured ice-cream, then add the fruit well-washed, peeled and cut into small pieces. Top with raspberry syrup. To compete add a spoonful of stoned black cherries in syrup. Serve.

PANERA

SERVES 4

50 gr. ground coffee
1 l liquid cream
30 gr. sugar
8 egg yolks

Combine all the ingredients and mix. Pour the cream mixture in a saucepan and allow to thicken over very low heat. Do not boil. Once thickened, remove and serve.

PANERA (ALTERNATE RECIPE)

SERVES 4

100 gr. Coffee
2 litres thickened cream
400 gr. sugar

Use coarse ground coffee; ground coffee used for espresso coffee is too fine, have coffee ground to required fineness. Combine coffee and thickened cream in saucepan, stir constantly. Bring to boil, add sugar and stir with wooden spoon until sugar is dissolved. Remove from heat, let stand until coffee deposits on sauacepan bottom. Filter, using strainer, and serve.

SWEET BREAD
PANDOLCE
SERVES 4

500 gr. flour
1 small glass Marsala wine
1 tbsp orange scented water
130 gr. sugar
30 gr. pistachio nuts
30 gr. candied fruit
40 gr. fresh yeast
120 gr. butter
10 gr. wild fennel seeds
30 gr. pine-nuts
30 gr. raisins
Butter and flour for oven tray

Place pistachio nuts in salted water for a couple of minutes to facilitate peeling of skin. Place raisins in small bowl of warm water to soften. Dice candied squash. With half the flour quantity make a mound on the work surface, add fresh yeast, a pinch of salt and a little warm water. Knead to make a smooth soft dough. Place in a bowl, covered with a thick cloth and put in a warm place to rest for at least a day. The following day, make mound with remaining flour on the work surface. Make well in centre an add the Marsala wine, the melted butter, a tbsp of orange scented water an sugar for last.
Mix all the ingredients well, then add the leavened dough of the previous day and knead thoroughly for at least half an hour. Add the fennel seeds, the pine-nuts, the shelled pistachio nuts, raisings and candied squash. Shape into a large, round loaf and place it onto a greased and floured baking tray. Around the loaf place ovenproof cardboard, about 10 cm. high, and staple to hold it firm. Cut crosswise slits on top of loaf, cover with cloth an let rest for about 10 hours in a warm place. Pre-heat oven to 180°C and bake the sweet bread for an hour. Remove from oven, leave to cool, remove carton "girdle" and serve.

SWEET BREAD (ALTERNATE RECIPE)
PANDOLCE
SERVES 4

1 kg. flour
250 gr. butter
400 gr. raisings
100 gr. pine-nuts
Vanilla essence
300 gr. sugar
2 eggs + 4 yolks
300 gr. candied fruit
1 small packet of yeast
2 tbsp honey

Make a mound with flour, place yeast and vanilla essence along mound side. Make well in centre and add the yolks, honey, softened butter and knead together. If dough is not elastic add a little water. Knead until dough is smooth, gradually add the raisins, pine-nuts and candied fruit. Mix thoroughly and then knead. Divide into 2 or 3 loaves and place onto greased oven trays. Pre-heat oven to 220°C and bake for about 1 hour. Let cool.

STUFFED PEACHES
PESCHE RIPIENE
SERVES 4

9 peaches
50 gr. candied squash
4-5 tbsp white wine
50 gr. candied citron
20 gr. sugar
Slab of butter

Split the peaches, sash and remove kernel. Finely chop candied citron and squash, add the peach flesh and a couple of tbsp of white wine. Spoon the mixture into the peach halves and arrange the split peaches onto a lightly greased tray. Sprinkle with sugar and bake in moderately hot oven (180°C) for half an hour and serve hot or cold.

SACRIPANTINA

Serves 4

200 gr. butter
A small glass espresso coffee
25 gr. dry liqueur
500 gr. sponge cake
4 plain biscuits
180 gr. Icing sugar
1/2 glass dry liqueur
25 gr. bitter cocoa
1 glass dry Marsala wine
3 almond cookies

Crush biscuits and almond cookies finely until powder. Mix with 30 gr of icing sugar. Split the sponge cake into 6 layers the size of the cake tin. In a bowl work butter with spoon until soft, add 150 gr sugar and mix. Ad the coffee, a tbsp at a time and then the liqueur. Dive the mixture into two parts and add the bitter cocoa to one of the parts. Cover a round cake tin with cellophane then place one of the layers of cake in the cake tin. Brush with Marsala wine and spread a third of the cocoa cream evenly over the cake. Place another layer of cake on top, brush again with dry Marsala wine and spread the coffee cream. Place a third layer of cake, brush again with dry Marsala wine and more cocoa cream. Continue this process alternating cocoa and coffee cream. Cut a round piece of cardboard slightly smaller in size than the cake tin, cover it with aluminium alfoil and place it on top of the cake layer. Place a weight on this cover and put in fridge for at least 3 hours.

Once removed from fridge, remove weight and carton disc and turn cake upside down on serving dish. Cover sides of cake with remaining cocoa cream, sprinkle the crumbed biscuits on top of cake. Refrigerate till served.

WALNUT CAKE
TORTA DI NOCE
SERVES 4

500 gr. walnuts
200 gr. flour
200 gr. sugar
1 egg
2 dl liquid cream
100 gr. candied fruit
Breadcrumbs
Slab butter

Shell nuts, blend with sugar, add an egg yolk, the whipped cream, candied fruit and fold in flour. Pre-heat oven to 150°C, grease and sprinkle bread-crumbs in baking tin, pour in mixture and bake for 45 minutes.

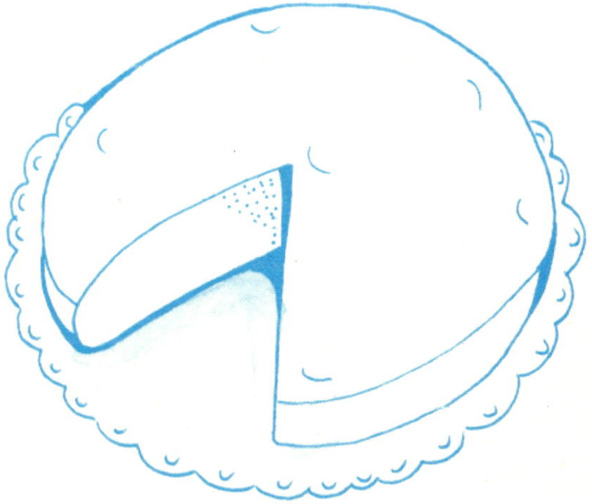

Indice

Finito di stampare
nel mese di maggio 2010
presso Ditta Giuseppe Lang - Genova

€7,90